African Magic Series

VODUN

WEST AFRICA'S SPIRITUAL LIFE

MONIQUE JOINER SIEDLAK

Oshun
Publications

Vodun: West Africa's Spiritual Life © Copyright 2021 by Monique Joiner Siedlak

ISBN: 978-1-950378-63-0

All rights reserved

The content contained within this book may not be reproduced, duplicated or transmitted without direct written permission from the author or the publisher.

Under no circumstances will any blame or legal responsibility be held against the publisher, or author, for any damages, reparation, or monetary loss due to the information contained within this book, either directly or indirectly.

Legal Notice

This book is copyright protected. It is only for personal use. You cannot amend, distribute, sell, use, quote or paraphrase any part, or the content within this book, without the consent of the author or publisher.

Disclaimer Notice

Please note the information contained within this document is for educational and entertainment purposes only. All effort has been executed to present accurate, up to date, reliable, complete information. No warranties of any kind are declared or implied. Readers acknowledge that the author is not engaged in the rendering of legal, financial, medical or professional advice. The content within this book has been derived from various sources. Please consult a licensed professional before attempting any techniques outlined in this book.

By reading this document, the reader agrees that under no circumstances is the author responsible for any losses, direct or indirect, that are incurred as a result of the use of the information contained within this document, including, but not limited to, errors, omissions, or inaccuracies.

Cover Design by MJS

Cover Image by AndreyCherkasov@depositphotos.com

Published by Oshun Publications

www.oshunpublications.com

Other Books in the Series

African Spirituality Beliefs and Practices
Hoodoo
Seven African Powers: The Orishas
Cooking for the Orishas
Lucumi: The Ways of Santeria
Voodoo of Louisiana
Haitian Vodou
Orishas of Trinidad
Connecting With Your Ancestors
Black Magic
The Orishas

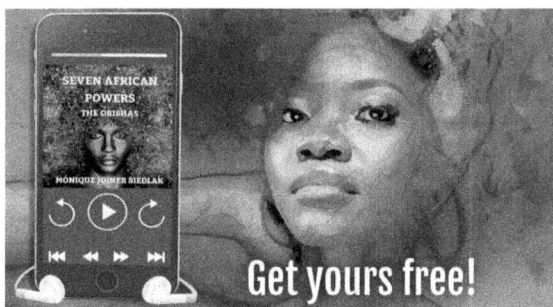

Get yours free!

Want to learn about African Magic, Wicca, or even Reiki while cleaning your home, exercising, or driving to work? I know it's tough these days to simply find the time to relax and curl up with a good book. This is why I'm delighted to share that I have books available in audiobook format.

Best of all, you can get the audiobook version of this book or any other book by me for free as part of a 30-day Audible trial.

Members get free audiobooks every month and exclusive discounts. It's an excellent way to explore and determine if audiobook learning works for you.

If you're not satisfied, you can cancel anytime within the trial period. You won't be charged, and you can still keep your book. To choose your free audiobook, visit:

www.mojosiedlak.com/audiobooks

WANT UPDATES, FREEBIES & GIVEAWAYS?!

MONIQUE JOINER SIEDLAK

THE ORISHAS

JOIN MY NEWSLETTER!

mojosiedlak.com/newsletter-signup

Contents

Introduction

In this book, we are going to talk about different aspects of Western African spirituality. I assume you have some knowledge of African spirituality, but you are curious to learn more. This book can also serve as a jumping-off point while engaging in the culture.

The main focus here is West African Vodun and its derivatives. I made this decision as I believe it is one of the Western African traditions' most substantial illustrations. Yoruba's religion is much more popular, and there is a lot of information made available to the public. It wouldn't be near as fun or intriguing as a case study, so you will find many free form discussions of the Yoruba religion. This is because the Yoruba have a close history with Benin's people and have similar spiritual ideas and practices. This makes their religion an exciting place to compare, contrast, and analyze.

You will find African spirituality to be diverse and freeing. These religions have a simultaneously releasing and immersive view of the world and its nature. While they govern many aspects of a person's life, they do not come with the kind of baggage, cynicism, and indeterminism that come with religions like Christianity or Catholicism.

What you can expect to find in the following chapters are:

- A discussion on the origins of West African stories and implications.
- A discussion of gods and goddesses and their roles within the Universe and life.
- We will talk a little about West African metaphysics, specifically how they make sense of the physical and spiritual world.
- We will define the role of God in the lives of people as shown in West African religions.
- We will tell stories of the gods and goddess and their significance for us and the faith as a whole.
- We will discuss ancestral spirits, rituals, and customs related to them and worship.
- Ancestral spirits concepts of death and the afterlife.
- How Vodun adherents choose who to worship, its traditions, attitudes of its supporters, and the nature of its ceremonies.
- The curious cultural and societal aspects of these West African communities.

West Africa is home to over 380 million people. It is made up of 16 countries whose history is closely inter-twined, with very few exceptions. Nine of its largest cities are in three countries: Nigeria, Ghana, and the Ivory Coast. West Africa boasts a diversity of ethnicities and cultures, the largest races in Yoruba, Igo, Fulani, Akan, and Wolof. The people of West Africa mainly speak non-Bantu Niger-Congo languages.

Although there are large groups of Christians in the region, Islam is the dominant religion reaching over 60% of West Africa. Traditional West African faiths are the oldest in the area with historical and cultural significance (Mbiti, 1994). The most significant religions being Akan, Yoruba, Odinani, and Sere. Vodun is practiced by 11% of the people of Benin (Folly, 2020). It is also found in many neighboring countries and the Americas in different versions. Still, these are mainly consistent with each other.

ONE

The Supreme Being

HERE WE WILL LOOK AT DIFFERENT SUPREME BEING concepts in West African religion, including their stories and roles. A clearer picture will emerge as we get further along, but first, let's cover the basics.

A Supreme Being refers to a creator, God, or the Universe's ultimate source and existence in the simplest terms. In the Western Hemisphere, we simply understand this as God. Like God, the Supreme Being has many common characteristics we know about a God, like omnipotence and omniscience. There are similarities in the majority of West African religions, but there are some defining differences. For instance, the Supreme Being is more deist. The everyday ruling and governing of the Universe are done through lesser deities or gods that he has created or emanated from him (God: African Supreme Beings, n.d.). Whereas for us, God is considered an intervening presence heavily invested in the world's affairs and mankind. Here we can start to see a different picture emerge.

One might be tempted to think the deities that function under Supreme Beings are analogous to Christianity's concepts of angels, spirits, and other forces, but that is inaccurate. Spirits such as angels presumably act under the direction of God with a specific purpose or goal for mankind. The Christian idea of God is decidedly ruler-like and why he is compared to a king. This is not as obvious in most West African religions. Here there is a vast chasm between the Supreme Being, his creation, and all other divinities in the Universe not directly under the Supreme Being's influence. Some West African religions where the Supreme Being plays more of a definitive role in its followers' lives. But most do not, and followers usually don't even directly worship the Supreme Being.

At this point, you might be asking yourself what is the point of worship or religion if God is uninvolved in the lives of his creation. The answer is: because of the absence of the Supreme Being, there is a deep need in people to find a spiritual home (God: African Supreme Beings, n.d.). This absence causes a pang of hunger and yearning for the supernatural. The divinities that interact with Earth affect the living. Life is considered a spiritual journey that can be aided by them, making sense to worship and follow these gods.

Think of the Universe, how incomprehensibly large it is, and all that is encompassed within it. We exist on a planet, part of a massive solar system, part of a vast galaxy, which is part of a more extensive collection of galaxies that are a slice of something exponentially bigger. There are more stars in the Universe than grains of sand on all of the world's beaches (more than sextillion). There are about two trillion galaxies in the Universe that we know of, and likely even more. When you think of something like that, of how powerful and incomprehensible a being would need to be to create it all, it becomes obvious why they would remain distant. They are far away, beyond comprehension. It would seem a direct interaction with us would be fruitless because we would barely hope to understand something magnificent (West African Religions, n.d.). No one could–at least that is how West African religions see it. Not in these words exactly but with the same meaning. So, the Supreme Being is something that the entire existence depends on, revered while still remaining shrouded in mystery.

Other gods can function as intermediaries between the Supreme Being and humans when necessary, or they can be worshiped for the favors they bring. Here we have a pantheon of gods with the Supreme Being as the ultimate source, functioning to maintain existence.

We have spoken of the Supreme Beings' distance to humanity; however, they are closely linked to nature: mountains, hills, trees, oceans, the sun, and the moon. Nature is seen as a direct presentation of the Supreme Being's presence and power. In this element, they are generally conceived as good, even with all the chaos and evil in the Universe from creation. This might seem contradictory, but chaos allows for free will and some Universe determinism (West African Religions, n.d.). The other spiritual beings are given some responsibilities in the Universe, and they might decide to do the wrong things for some reason or another. West Africans do not believe that the Supreme Being is directly responsible for all that goes wrong globally; to them, the Supreme Being is blameless or neutral. West African religions construe deities and other spirits in direct contact with human beings responsible for the bad. In some cases, they may try to turn to the Supreme Being for help when other spirits are not heeding their prayers.

Now, let's explore how each West African religion depicts the Supreme Being.

Dogon of Mali

Amma is the Supreme Being of the Dogon people of Mali; he is credited with creating everything. This is a more active, hands-on approach than any of the other Supreme Beings we will discuss. It is reminiscent of an Abrahamic God in that way, but more fractured and unusual.

It starts with Amma creating the heavens and the Earth using sacred utterances. He made nature, and then he built a sacred granary and rum, which are symbols of culture and communications. Amma is depicted in the shape of an egg with four collarbones that divide the shape. Each quarter represents one of the four elements: earth, fire, air, and water (God: African Supreme Beings, n.d.).

To create human beings, Amma put a seed within himself and used seven utterances to make the seed grow and into the image of a man (God: African Supreme Beings, n.d.). Amma produced male and female twins by dividing the egg into a double placenta and placing them inside. They are directly from Amma, so they are considered his children. Yurugu broke from the placenta, looking to mate with a woman and recreate Amma's creation. A piece of the broken placenta became the earth. When Yurugu could not find someone like him to mate with, he did so with the Earth, his mother. There is no retelling or evidence of what remained of the female twin.

This soiled the earth, and Amma worked to restore creation. To mend it, Amma made a male twin named Nommo and created four more spirits from him. Those four spirits are considered ancestors of the Dogon people.

The four spirits and Dogon descended to earth in an ark filled with all the things they needed to restore the world to purity. With them, light and rain came. Through them, we have humanity, animals, plants, and all life on earth. Yurugu's behavior caused darkness, sterility, and death, and Nommo balances this by bringing light, rain, and fertility. Dogon people think of Yurugu as personifying all that is undesirable, inhabitable, or unfriendly, while Nommo is the negating force. It is one of the few openly dualistic religions in West Africa. Although good and evil concepts exist in other faiths, those depictions are not necessarily baked in creation stories. Some are considered amoral.

Another version of the creation story is concerned with explaining human psychology and behavior. Amma is lonely after he makes heavenly bodies and is aroused by the earth. So he mates with the Earth. The result of this is a pair of green-colored half-humans and serpents with the divine essence. It is thought that these beings are the source of all human behavior.

It is strange, complex, and confusing; at the center of it is procreation as a massive power, even without intercourse. For instance, take the symbol or shape of Amma as an egg, which denotes sexuality or the reproductive system even in its absence.

Akan People of Ghana

The Supreme Being of the Akan people is called Nyame (Nyonmo, Nyama, or Nyam). It comes from the Akan word meaning 'to be full' or 'satisfied.' This is interpreted from the saying, "if you get him, you are satisfied." The name also comes from the root word nyam, which means shining, glory, or brightness (God: African Supreme Beings, n.d.). To the Akan, all these things describe the Supreme Being.

The Akan do not have a very detailed origin story, but they credit Nyame with all creation. It is believed that Nyame created the sky before he created the Earth, rivers, waters, plants, and trees. After all this, he saw the earth was ready for a man, so he made the first man, Okane, and the first woman, Kyeiwaa. They lived in a cave where Nyame taught them the names of everything in existence.

Nyame imposes and gives structure to all societies, animals, and plants. Nyame has deities called children since they get their powers from him.

Nyame's praise name is Odomankoma, and his title is Borebore, which means hewer, excavator, creator, originator, inventor, or architect (God: African Supreme Beings, n.d.).

Mende of Sierra Leone

The Mende call their Supreme Being Ngewo. The name is thought to come from ngele, which means sky, and woo, which means long ago, meaning "in the sky, from long ago." They think of their Supreme Being in masculine terms, referring to him as the father. He also goes by the name Leve, meaning "the giver of chicken" or "the high one." They consider Ngewo as being high up in the sky, far away, and at the same time, everywhere (God: African Supreme Beings, n.d.).

Like the Supreme Being before, Ngewo is credited with creating the Universe and all that is in it. He controls the Universe. The Mende people credit Ngewo with their overall wellbeing, victory over enemies, successful revenge, and protection. This is an example of a Supreme Being in the West African religion, which is regarded as being more involved in his creations' lives.

It is said that Ngewo created the earth and all things before making a man and woman. In this story, Ngewo is anthropomorphized as a spirit in a cave with a door. He was so powerful that the words he uttered became a reality. There came a day when Ngewo said, "I have all this power, why don't I use it? I have lived alone for a long time with no one to talk to and no one to play with. I want all kinds of animals to live with me in this cave," and that's how animals were created (God: African Supreme Beings, n.d.).

Through his power, the animals came in pairs. He closed the door, gave the animals rules that would govern their living, and warned them that violations had terrible consequences. The first law was food. He said to the animals, "I will give you anything you want to eat, but you must not touch my food" (God: African Supreme Beings, n.d.). After this, Ngewo looked at the cave and thought it was small, so he expanded it. Doing so made the food in the cave bigger, which delighted the animals. Ngewo was very happy as he had friends to talk and play with.

One day one of the animals visited Ngewo and smelled something delicious. The animal found the food he smelled and ate some. Ngewo teleported the animal to him immediately, and the animal was confused in front of the powerful being. He said to the animal, "What brought you here? You have violated my law" (God: African Supreme Beings, n.d.). Ngewo then threw the animal out of the cave in rage and said, "You! From now on, your name is cow" (God: African Supreme Beings, n.d.).

This is the same story for all animals; thrown out and named. The first couple was called Ngewo Maad-le, which means "He is the grandfather." Ngewo told them if they ask anything, he will give it to them, including food. This is consistent with that point about Ngewo being a more involved Supreme Being. They requested things from Ngewo by saying, "Maada, give us this," or "Maada, give us that" (God: African Supreme Beings, n.d.). Ngewo replied: "In ngee," which means 'take it.'

But, as you might imagine, Ngewo grew tired of them only coming to ask for things. So he decided to leave. Saying, "If I stay near these people, they will wear me with their requests; I will make another living place for myself far above them" (God: African Supreme Beings, n.d.). They woke up one day, and Ngewo was no longer there. They looked up at the heavens and saw him spread out in the sky. He ascended further, away from animals and humans, where he continues his watch over his food.

The Mende pray to Ngewo and regard him as their creator and the one who is ultimately responsible for them. It makes sense when you think of this story; he plays the role of caretaker and can come back to Earth anytime he wants. The Mende use ancestors, which we will talk about later, as intermediaries to speak to Ngewo.

Yoruba of Nigeria

Yoruba's Supreme Being is Olodumare, also referred to as Olorun, which means "one who owns or resides in the sky" (God: African Supreme Beings, n.d.). He is also credited with creating the world and is omnipotent.

Olodumare works through hundreds of lower gods called orishas. The exact number of orishas changes depending on who you speak to; some say 201, and others believe there are 401. They share the same substance or essence as Olodumare, who delegates specific aspects of the

Universe for them to maintain. This is thought to allow the Universe to stabilize along with the everyday world of human beings. All orishas have authority over these elements, while others are charged with maintaining order and morality within humanity.

The creation story of Olodumare is complex. It involves Obatala, one of the oldest and prominent orishas. Olodumare gave him dry soil, a five-toed hen, and a chameleon. Obatala dropped the dry soil to the primordial water surface, and the hen spread the mud on the surface of the water. The chameleon is there to test if the earth is now a livable place and reports to Olodumare, who gives Obatala instructions to take clay and mold humans. At the same time, Olodumare breathes life into the clay figure.

The relationship between Olodumare and the divinities reveals much of his nature. We will learn more about this as we explore Vodun, as it shares many similarities with Yoruba's religion.

Fon of Benin

The Supreme Being of the Fon is Nana Buluku. Nana Bulku made everything that exists, and she gave birth to two gods named Mawu and Lisa. Mawu is a moon spirit, considered a secondary creator, and Lisa is the sun spirit. Nana Buluku is consistent with the deistic aspects of the West African Supreme Being. After she made the Universe and gave birth to these two spirits, she left everything to them.

Mawu created the world by shaping it into a lower bowl and making the sky a lid. She traveled with a large snake called Aido-Hwedo, whose movements on the earth shaped the earth: valleys, mountains, and other natural occurring formations. When Mawu saw that the world was sinking under its weight. She had her snake wrap around the Earth to hold it in place.

Mawu would assist in the making of all life on earth. She asked a monkey called Awe to help make more animals out of clay. Given this much power, the monkey became arrogant and started to boast to other animals, thinking they were gods. The first woman created by Mawu saw the damage this was causing. She told her children to go out in the world and tell people that only Mawu can give the breath of life (synonymous with Mawu is the true god). Awe climbed up to the heavens trying to prove that he is just as powerful as Mawu, but he failed. Mawu made him a bowl of porridge and put the seed of death in it to show him she is the only one who can give life and take it.

Mawu and Lisa would create and give birth to other divinities, which we will look at in the upcoming sections. In some iterations, Mawu and Lisa are not considered consorts but two sides of the same entity. The deities that descend from them are called Vodun.

What Is the Significance?

These stories are creative ways of telling us about how the world functions, its origins, and how humans fit in that world. As we explore more details, we can provide more answers. Now, let us examine those claims to tease out the meaning and why we should care.

Origins and Nature of the World

These stories answer questions of where the Universe comes from by invoking the Supreme Being. But a more subtle point is present: dependents can't exist on their own.

We are dependent on plants, animals, water, and other

ideal conditions for existence. Animals depend on plants, plants depend on the sun and soil, the earth depends on gravity, etc. If I kept going, you would realize there has to be one thing that depends on only itself, and everything else falls in line. That is the Supreme Being or God in this situation. In philosophical terms, it is called a necessary being because, without it, nothing can be, so it stands to reason that everything comes from it (Peter Van Inwagen, 2015). This answers the question of where the Universe comes from, but it also implies the nature of the Universe. That it is dependent, and there is no strong separation between the Supreme Being and the Universe because the latter could not exist without the former.

This is a significant point because, in the western world, we are used to thinking of the world having spiritual things and material things. This reflects a limit of our human abilities; it does not say anything about how the world is. The Universe does not contain things that are either spiritual or physical; all things in it are made of the same essence/energy. Spiritual things and physical things aren't fundamentally different. There are just words we use to categorize and explain our experience.

Spirits exist, not separate from and alien to reality. They interact with the world in a way that is every bit as influential and essential as physical things because they are all part of the same Universe. Human beings at the fundamental level are spiritual beings. Still, our world experience makes us mostly blind to spiritual forces that exist among us and influence our world.

Our Place in the World

Through these stories, we learn of the beginning of man. They come from the Supreme Being; they are a direct result of the Supreme Being's activities. This makes us unique, but because of the Supreme Being's deistic nature, we know we are not the center of the Universe or the only thing that matters.

This reveals a profound truth about humanity. It confirms that we are at the mercy of forces incomprehensibly more powerful than ourselves and how, despite it all, we can live fulfilling lives by co-opting those powerful forces. The stories act as a manual on how to survive and thrive in a mostly unpredictable, cold, and challenging world. And as we will see, they tell us about our ultimate destination as a species. How we can transcend limitations, reach our higher selves, and attain spiritual awakening.

Solving Difficult Questions

The deistic nature of West African religions avoids difficult theological questions. We will look briefly at one and how it is explained by the West African views of the Supreme Being.

On the Origins of Evil

One of the most challenging problems of Abrahamic conceptions of God is the problem of evil. Simply stated, the question is, "If God is good and all-powerful, why does he allow evil in the world?" Three options can be put to this: God is not all-powerful, God is not good, or God does not exist. Philosophers and theologians have tested this in several ways.

One of the options is that God allows evil in the world because if he didn't, we wouldn't have free will. The idea is that God gave us free will, and that would be meaningless if our only choice was to be good. Any meaningful idea of free will allows us to choose evil if we please. The free will answer suggests evil exists precisely because God is good and gave us free will. More than that, why didn't he make a world where we could choose evil but had better self-control or determination over our lives? A world where we could choose evil, but we were raised in relatively positive environments that didn't do untold damage to our psyche or our ability to make the right decisions—a more equal world. Even if we accepted this answer, it does not explain why there is suffering in the world.

Natural evil is the senseless suffering we see in the world that does not intentionally stem from humanity. It's the little girl with terminal cancer and the earthquake that kills millions. These types of tragedies have nothing to do with free will. They are simply examples of suffering and evil. Why would a loving, all-powerful God build a world capable of torment? Even if they happen less frequently, they are still hurtful things that shouldn't exist.

Philosophers and theologians try to explain the problem of natural evil with the idea that God, being all-powerful, must have made the best possible world. Maybe if God had built any other planet, it would be more terrible than this one. Also, these tragedies allow us to act in ways that are honorable and noble. The problem with this answer is that it is not convincing. One can imagine a world where there is no suffering. Still, there is good suffering that allows people to do honorable and noble things. Good tolerable suffering could be having a curable disease, which is painful, allowing others to act in heroic ways.

Or another example would be losing all of your money but not dying poor and miserable by allowing others to offer charity. In other words, it does not have to be bad. It makes God out to be someone who is playing games or not as intelligent or imaginative as we think he is.

Another option is that bad things happen with good

underlying reasons, usually beyond our observation. This would lead us to believe that there is more senseless suffering in the world than needs to be. We can calculate the probability that something terrible is happening for reasons beyond our knowledge. With this reasoning, there would be four possibilities for or every instance of senseless suffering:

1. The bad is happening for no reason.
2. The bad is happening for a good reason unknown to us.
3. The bad is happening for a bad reason unknown to us.
4. The bad is happening for reasons we know. In other words, there is no additional unknown reason.

Note: We can't add an option that says what appears to be unnecessary suffering has a good reason to observe because it wouldn't be an instance of senseless suffering.

As you can see, this leaves us with a one in four chance that any instance of senseless suffering is happening for a good reason. If you were a betting person, I don't think you would take those odds. So, believers, philosophers, and theologians seem to be stuck with a riddle they can't crack. The problem of evil can't be explained away by Satan or evil spirits because, in the end, those things were created by a supposedly good being that is all-powerful but somehow made a world where all these bad things can happen.

For West African religions like Vodun, these problems disappear. Their conception of God is deistic. The Supreme Being is not interested in what goes on in his creation. In some cases, the Supreme Being is not even responsible for creating the world or humans. A God like that can let all sorts of things happen in the world because he is indifferent to it all. It might even be that they dislike their creation. A God like that is neither good nor bad. They just are. Their most important function is that they hold the Universe together. Our job is to make our lives as meaningful as we can with whatever tools we can find and hope the gods are on our side.

TWO

Deities in West African Vodun

VODUN IS A RELIGION OF THE FON PEOPLE OF DAHOMEY kingdom, modern-day Benin. The word Vodun comes from the Fon word that means spirit or god. When enslaved people were taken to Haiti and other regions in the Americas, many brought Vodun with them. They would combine with Catholic lithography, rites, and practices to hide it from their masters. So you will find different versions of Vodun in other parts of America and Western Africa.

Vodun practitioners refer to their deities, Mawu and Lisa's descendants, as vodun or loa (sometimes lwa). The loa are the ones who intervene in human affairs, guide, praise and punish. They can also bring healing and other benefits.

Vodun emphasizes the interconnectedness of things in the Universe. Sickness and other problems are caused by blockages that impede or stop energy flow, which is what the world and body need to maintain proper health. In the Vodun practice, everything has to stay changing, moving, and vibrant allowing for harmony, peace, healing, survival, and a communal spirit. In this framework, respect for elders, justice, serving the community, charity, patience, and empathy are expected from believers. It ties in with Vodun's ethos for unity and interconnectedness of the forces. In other words, things that sow conflict, separate, and fracture relations are the antithesis of Vodun beliefs. All things connect, and people should work towards maintaining and keeping that connection: connection to the living and the dead, the earth, land, spirits, water, peace, and rhythm (Vodun (Voodoo), n.d.).

Vodun also has a place for ancestral beliefs. The idea that when our loved ones die, they pass on to another realm, become spirits that protect and guide us, and communicate with the gods on our behalf.

In this chapter, we will look at the different Vodun and their roles. There is much more Vodun than those that are listed here. We will look at other versions of the same spirits from the Yoruba religion. This is intentional as the Yoruba conquered the Fon people and adopted some of the Fon beliefs and practices.

Xevioso: Vodun of Thunder

Xevioso is the child of Mawu and Lisa. He is the god or lord of thunder. A god of thunder is one of the most common in cultures around the world. In Yoruba's version, he is considered the strongest. He represents wrath, aggression, and punishment. In other words, Xevioso is understood as primarily a spirit of explosive, uncontrollable emotion like anger, violence, and tremendous power. This is a double-edged sword as he can protect those who honor him, but if they offend him in any way, he will likely turn on them.

This is the spirit you turn to when you are looking for justice. Still, anger is usually a sign that something isn't as it should be, or there has been a violation of some agreement or law. In my opinion, this is a clearer image of Xevioso.

In most cases, spirits host and govern over the earth, and there is a set of agreements we have towards one another: a type of an unspoken agreement. We go into the world having agreed on a particular set of rules like not stealing from or hurting each other, and so forth. And when someone steals from us, we feel violated, and we have a right to be angry about it, even more so if we know they are getting away with it. Your anger is a sign that someone is not playing by the rules—an injustice has been done. Given this, it is not illogical to suggest that exercising your anger would restore justice and, therefore, balance the world. In other words, Xevioso is the protector and dispenser of justice. Through his acts, he enforces and keeps relations between the gods in check and us. It is not senseless, aimless, unexplainable anger, or fury. Although we may not understand it sometimes, it adds up on a cosmic scale.

Sakpata: Vodun of Earth

When Mawu was dividing the world between her children, Sakpata was given dominion over the earth, at the displeasure of his sister Sogbo. Sakpata came down from heaven with plants, crops, tools, and skills that humans could use for development. Because he had taken so much with him, he did not have space for other necessary elements like water and fire, which were stolen later.

Humans were excited when Sakpata descended from the heavens with these tools of wealth. There was a lot of promise in them, and they hoped they would see their lives improve. Legba, Sakpata's youngest sibling, told Sogbo, who was given control of the skies, to withhold rain in the sky. Knowing that their mother noticed, Legba went to Mawu and told her water would not be enough for everyone on earth, including the plants. Alarmed, Mawu ordered Legba to tell Sogbo to withhold the rains, which he had already done.

Sakpata soon realized that his crops needed rain, but none came. A drought ensued that caused everything to become dry and brittle. Humans began getting angry with Sakpata. They harassed him and cursed him for lying to them about the prosperity and convenience he had promised. Legba came down and found his brother in a messy state. That was when he told Sakpata he would talk to Mawu on his behalf. He told Sakpata to watch for a messenger, wututu bird, who would say to him what to do when the time came. When the bird returned, it told Sakpata to instruct the others to light a great fire, so the smoke could rise to heaven, signaling their distress.

Because it was so dry, everything caught fire very quickly, and the fire leaped into the sky. When Legba saw, he went to Mawu and told her that the earth was burning and the fire was so high and powerful it might spread to the heavens. Alarmed, Mawu told Legaba to order Sogbo to release the rain. The rain put out the flames and returned fertility to the land. It was decided that although Sogbo controlled the sky, people can call for rain when needed (Belcher, 2005).

What does this story reveal? In this context, it describes the role and power of the spirit of the earth, Sakpata. Sakpata is not the Vodun of Agriculture or fertility, but he is the god of progress and elevating society. When the spirit comes to rule over men, he brings them the tools of trade, crops they can domesticate, and abilities such as woodworking and carpentry skills. These are ways in which this spirit facilitates that mission of progress and growth by equipping humans with the capabilities to prosper, the right tools, and the right environment to do so.

This spirit works among humans within their communities to improve their lives. We are already beginning to see how interconnectedness and coming together works here because the spirit is multifaceted and uses various ways to meet the same end. While the title of Vodun of Earth denotes agriculture, it is wrong to think in these limited terms about Sakpata. Any role that he has in agriculture would be in service of progress.

Worshiping a spirit like this opens your eyes to how things in the world are interconnected, especially those things that propel us forward. You will begin to see its hands keeping things working together and moving towards greatness. This spirit will show you how disparaging moments can be shaped to better yourself through intermediaries or more direct routes in a more localized way.

I should point out, in some iterations of Vodun, Xeviosso is Sogbo, daughter of Mawu and Lisa.

Agbe: Vodun of the Sea

Agbe is the third-born son of Mawu and Lisa. He is the one who is given dominion over the seas and sea life. There aren't many stories based on Agbe, but as we look back to Mawu's creation of the world, Agbe's role within the world becomes obvious. When Mawu built the world, she was afraid that the earth would drown from the added weight, so her snake came in to save it. However, the waters can still be unpredictable, rough, and sometimes cause a whole host of problems.

The land is resting on an outline of great waters, waters that can engulf the land when disturbed. So Agbe functions to keep the waters at bay, provide safety, and protect from powerful storms. Agbe also has some effects on the land that the people experience. For instance, when earthquakes happen, they can be explained by his activity–he has made the water do something that makes the land shake. The serpent is primarily there to keep the world from sinking. The Fon being a fishing people, might have also worshipped Agbe for his luck.

So we see Agbe as the protector, provider, and calmer of seas. He's not the only one who performs these roles, but he is one of the most powerful to do so. Again, we see how together each god's roles feed on each other or strengthen each other. While Sakpata pushes for progress, Agbe is the one holding forces that threaten peace and the very land we live on intact.

You can pray to him for protection, maintenance, and calm in your life. These are, in a nutshell, where the spirit excels. But when displeased, it may be a source of chaos, destruction, especially the kind that upends people's lives. So he is a potent spirit. In my opinion much more influential than Xevioso, the Vodun of Thunder.

Gu: Vodun of Iron and War

They say Gu was born with a human body and a blade as a head (Belcher, 2005). This perfectly portrays his role as the god of iron and war. The two things are related; iron ore is used to make weapons for war, among other things.

A title like the Vodun of War denotes a spirit who is

angry or out for destruction or chaos, but that's false. A god of war is not necessarily there to sow conflict and division. Still, they are there to bestow victory, wisdom, and protection in battle when facing your enemies. Immediately we run into trouble. Why does he favor one side over another? These reasons are privy to him but always in the interest of ultimate fairness.

The Fon worshiped Gu to bring them success in war and protect them in conflicts, protect their wealth and community. At the end of the day, that is what a god of war is supposed to do—a more accurate title would-be protector of communities and nations.

There is also a building role. Iron is a symbol for minerals that can be mined and used to service those pursuits that strengthen and protect a nation. It stands for resources that can be used as weapons and defense. You can substitute nations with family, community, town, tradition, culture, city, or whatever you think is worthy of protection or strengthening. The Vodun of War resides over these matters. It dispenses favor, resources, wisdom, and advantage according to its divine wisdom and foresight.

Age: Vodun of Agriculture and the Forest

The Fon, borrowing elements from the Yoruba, tells a story of a hunter whose wife was ill with leprosy. The hunter went to the forest and heard the beating of drums, songs being sung, and the dance movement echoed throughout. He walked in the direction of the sounds curious and saw the agbui; these are bush spirits that look like rats. He listened as the rats sang about the world's history, how the first trees were made, then came the humans and animals. They sang about how they were the first of all the animals to be created and how much older they were than lions, leopards, and the other great beasts that roamed the earth. They chronicled how great birds were made like the eagle and hawk, and then creatures of the waters like fish and crocodiles came to be. "All these were sent by Mawu," they sang (Belcher, 2005).

At this time in the story, the people were sick, and many died. They did not yet know of medicine, cures, or treatments. The hunter's wife was one of the ill and wanted to search the forest for help. He eventually came upon a mound, like that of a mole, and found a spirit of the bush here, the azizañ. The spirit spoke to the hunter, and when the man told him about his wife, he offered a cure with special leaves. The hunter took them and used them to boil down and wash his wife with. She was cured.

People were shocked when they heard of this, so they began to come to him asking for cures and medicine. The spirit had told him he could come back whenever he needed a cure for any ailment. So when they came to him and begged for help, the hunter led them to the mound where the spirit lives. They would speak about their ailments, and the spirit would provide a cure.

Word of the spirit who lived in the forest and the hunter reached a king. The king went to the mound with an offering of a goat, liquor, and palm oil and told the spirit that they had no means of curing sickness in other parts of the country. The spirit gave the king many spirits who, when worshiped, would provide cures for ailments. Among them were the vodun Age, the Vodun of Agriculture, and the forest (Belcher, 2005).

This story tells us the role of Age. He is a god of nourishment and medicine, not only with plants to eat, but he provides safety on a hunt and protection in the forests. The story recalls a hunter because hunters are revered in many African cultures as intermediaries between this world and the spiritual world. They are seen as heroes of the community because they venture out, sometimes into danger, and bring wealth, knowledge, and wellness.

Putting Age in the same story as the discovery of medicine solidifies his position as providing knowledge and guidance about medicine. He offers plants and other healing properties. Putting him next to hunters solidifies his role as the one who blesses, favors. It protects hunters when they are out on the hunt, securing nourishment. As rural communities turned into farmers, he became sacred there too.

How should we perceive Age for our time? We understand Age as a god who provides nutrition and facilitates spiritual and physical aid. A god with wisdom, insight, and influence that can restore health. Age is a vodun you can turn to in times of hunger, sickness, and suffering.

Jo: Vodun of Air

Jo is the vodun of air, storms, winds, and weather. The Vodun of Air is worshiped because of the effect they have on important aspects of everyday life. They will affect the crops with powerful winds that can erode the soil and blow away nutrients that plants need to grow. Winds invite sandstorms that destroy buildings, property and sometimes cause death. These gods also provide the winds for travel. They can provide you with a cool breeze on a hot summer day. It's easy to see why people appease the air god when you think of all they are capable of.

What does this tell us about our relationship with the air god? Jo is the Vodun of Momentum. We know how they say when speed is with you, everything gets easier. This is how this vodun can serve you. It is much easier to go with the wind than against it. The people who turn to this spirit hope for calm, protection, and favor in their endeavors. This is how we can understand this god for our modern world situation outside of the effects and influence they have on nature.

Legba: Vodun of the Unpredictable

Legba is one of the most popular, complex vodun in the Dahomey Vodun religion. He is the last born of Mawu and Mawu's favorite. Interestingly, when Mawu divided the world between her children, she gave them all different languages, so they cannot communicate with each other. However, Legba was given the ability to speak in all tongues and function as an intermediary between the other entities and his mother. As we have seen in the story of Sakpata, Legba was the one who went back and forth between the different gods. If anyone wants to communicate with the gods, they must go through Legba because he understands all languages. Some iterations give other reasons why Legba is given these positions, things like he can play the gong, drums, flute, and bell while dancing. Legba's stories are many, and we will see how he functions within the Vodun pantheon as we go through one of them.

Because Legba can pass messages around, he is the servant of Fa. He is the god of divination in Vodun and the Yoruba's religion. Stories say that Legba would climb up a palm tree where Fa lived and opened her sixteen eyes following her instructions, enabling her to see.

There is one story that is thought to represent the quali-ties of Legba. Legba formed a band with his siblings: Aovi and Minona. Aovi is the god who punishes those who disrespect the gods, and Minona is the goddess who protects women. They traveled the land playing for funerals (a common custom), and they ended up meeting some influential people at one.

King Metonofi, the ruler of the dead, attended this funeral and was unhappy about his daughter marrying King Adja after discovering he was impotent. King Adjas's son was also at the funeral along with Fa, the spirit of divination. Fa is not able to speak, so he needs Legba to communicate on his behalf.

The King's son went to Fa to tell him about his father's impotence, asking the spirit to help him. This is not unusual within the Vodun religion as Fa diviners were considered for most problems. Fa instructed Legba to give the son a white powder that would enable him to consummate the marriage. Still, Legba gave the son a red powder that removes potency altogether.

Legba and his siblings played at the funeral and paid in cowrie-shells. They were traveling to another destination when they stopped to share the shells. The shells would not divide evenly between them, so they argued about who should get the extra pay. A woman walked by, and they asked her to decide who should get the remaining shell. The woman thought the eldest of the three should get the shell. The oldest was Minona. Aovi and Legba became furious. They killed the woman and threw her body in the bush and before Legba committed necrophilia.

Another woman passed by, they asked her who should get the remaining shell. She said the middle child should get it. She was killed by Legba and Minona. Legba lay with her dead body as well. The third woman they asked said the youngest should get the remaining shell. She was killed too, and Legba slept with her.

Seeing there was no convincing the siblings, Legba made a figure that looked like a dog and gave it the ability to move and speak. When the siblings saw it, they asked what they should do with the remaining shell. The dog told them to give it to their ancestors. The dog dug a hole, and the siblings put the remaining shell in it to be buried. This is meant to convey why animals deserve respect.

Many complained to King Metonofi and Fa about the women who were killed and the king's power. Metonofi sent for Legba, but Legba ran to his in-laws. His father-in-law was gone, so he slept in the same bed with his mother-in-law, with whom he had sex with her in the middle of the night. The next morning Legba was caught and brought before Metonoifi to answer for his actions. His father-in-law was also there, accusing Legba of adultery. They asked him about the three dead women. Legba said the other siblings were guilty of these crimes and saw no other way out except to make a figure of a dog to speak on his behalf.

Hearing this, Metonofi was impressed by the creativity Legba used to solve the problem. He awarded Legba the responsibility of watching over the people. Metonofi ordered Minona to become the protector of women. Hearing of Aovi's extraordinary violence, he gave him the responsibility of enforcing respect for the gods.

When that was settled, Legba's father-in-law brought his accusations before Metonofi. Legba said it was a mistake to sleep in the same bed as his mother-in-law. But Metonofi would not be persuaded by this plea and barred Legba from living among the humans. He would live only along roads and in desolate open spaces. This explains why shrines to Legba are placed at crossroads or town gates.

King Adja's complaint was that Legba had given them a red powder that made men impotent. Legba denied this, saying he had only mixed the white powder with blood and nothing wrong with it. When asked about the real red powder, he said he mixed it with clay.

Metonofi built a hut and placed his daughter inside. He ordered the men of Adja to attempt to have sex with her. One by one, they tried and failed because they had all taken the red powder that Legba had given them. Legba told them he would be able to do it and asked the people to play drums and sing. Legba entered the hut dancing and lay with Metonofi's daughter, who was a virgin. Dancing, Legba came out of the hut with his erect penis, bloodied to show that he had completed the task.

Metonofi then asked Legba to marry his daughter. Legba suggested that she be married to Fa and her name become Adje, which means cowries. At the wedding, Legba mixed the good powder in the wine and served it to all the guests, and the men soon recovered their ability to mate (Belcher, 2005).

This is a slightly more complex story that attempts to explain a lot about the other Fon gods, practices, and beliefs.

In Vodun statues, Legba is always portrayed as a male with an enormous erect penis. It is never fully explained where his insatiable thirst for sex comes from. To natives, it is a sign of fertility and symbolic of procreation. Legba is present in many versions of Vodun because of the central role he plays. In Haitian Vodou, he is referred to as Papa Legba. He is considered a great speaker who is playful and loves to fool others.

This story and the one of the Skapata and the drought illustrate how Legba outwits and tricks the other gods for his benefit or being funny. This trickery would not be possible if it wasn't for his language skills, wisdom, and forethought. This story illustrates these qualities by placing him in scenarios where he must rely on his ingenuity to escape or succeed.

Not much is spent explaining Legba's intentions. Legba is considered this way because he is Legba, not some overarching plan or goal. A trait that makes Legba unpredictable, a creature of his own passions and ultimately free. In so many ways, he is the most human and more likable than any of the gods. He has to be this way because he functions as a bridge between humans and the gods. Humans need to be able to relate to him and find him approachable.

In so many ways, he is the agent of change, always contorting and exploiting relations between humans and the gods, and also between the gods themselves, allowing Vodun to remain versatile and increasingly adaptable. This is why you will find that many people who believe in Vodun do not see a contradiction between themselves and Christianity or other religions. The Supreme Being may remain the same, but the smaller gods that inhabit their creation can change to fit the times. So these spirits will continue to manifest themselves in the world in ever-evolving, exciting ways through Legba. This is consistent with the religion's emphasis on dynamism.

People make offerings to Legba and worship him because he is the one most known within the pantheon. In other words, he can get you almost anything you want because he is the smartest, most influential god. This explains why he is so ubiquitous and revered among believers.

THREE

Ancestral Spirits

I HAVE SPOKEN OF WEST AFRICAN RELIGIONS NOT HAVING A
clear separation between the physical and spiritual world–
both being of the same essence and mostly occupying the
same space. A clear example of this is their belief in ancestral spirits.

In West African religions and plenty of other African
religions, they don't immediately leave our world when they
die. They simply transcend to another level of existence,
becoming the living dead. These spirits are usually people
who are considered to have lived a good life. This is
primarily determined by their relationship with family,
wealth, and age at death. These spirits are considered
prominent parts of the community and contain vast knowledge about the past and the future. They can guide their
family or entire community by urging them to uphold
specific standards and imparting wisdom. These spirits
must be treated with respect and honored regularly.

The power of ancestral spirits comes from the gods, and
they function under their authority. They may be given

specific influence in particular areas like arts, business, farming, and more. But they can never work alone or against the gods. It is helpful to think of them as the most influential members of West African communities and direct servants of the gods.

The ancestors can be honored in various ways. They can be honored by pouring libation, which gives them the first taste of a drink. They also accept chicken and goat sacrifices, kola, or nuts. Worshipers can also act in ways that the spirits would find pleasing, which ties in with upholding specific ethical standards for the community and individual.

Egungun

Egungun is a masquerade that is practiced to venerate the ancestors. In these festivals, trained ancestral communicators or family elders wear elaborate costumes and dance to drums. During this time, they can become possessed with ancestral spirits. Through this, they are considered to cleanse the community and allow the spirits to inhabit the societies they watch over for a time. During which they can communicate to the gathered about a variety of things. In the end, the practitioners give the collected messages, blessings, and warnings as directed by the ancestral spirits. In this way, the ancestors are being appeased, invited into the community, and allowed to speak to the community's direction.

To understand why they would perform this ceremony and why it works, we need to look at how the Yoruba makes sense of death and life. The Yoruba tells the following story to illustrate when a man defeated death by using only a mask.

"Long, long ago, Death (ikui) and his followers regularly

invaded Ife. Every fourth day they came from heaven to the Ojaife market, where they killed as many people as possible with the staff that Death had given them. Eventually, most of the people of Ife were destroyed. Those who remained cried to Lafogido, who was then Qni, and to Odua, Orisanla, Orisa Ijugbe, Oriis Alase, and all the orisa to save them. But the orisa could do nothing to drive these spirits away. Finally, Amaiyegun promised to save them. He brought colored cloths, which he sewed into a costume that completely covered his body. The outfit's arms were like gloves to fit his fingers, and the legs of the costume like gloves to fit his toes. He sacrificed a ram, a cock, and three whips (ifin) in making the costume.

Then he called the people to him. First, he put his left foot into the costume's leg, which came up to the knee. Then he showed it to the people, and they began to sing: 'Come and see the foot, a fine secret.' He put his right leg into the costume and extended it so that the people could see. They sang the song again. He put his left arm and then his right arm into the outfit. Each time (the people sang): 'Come and see the hand, a fine secret.' Finally, he put on the gown which covered his face and entire body.

He took off the costume and stored it away in his room. When he found that Death would come again the next day, he went to the Qni and promised he would save the people on the morrow. In the morning (Amaiyegun) and his follow- ers, who did not wear costumes, went to the Ojaife market and hid in the large trees' buttresses. Soon the townspeople began to come to the market. Not long afterward, Death and his followers descended on them, killing them with their staff. Amaiyegun came out from his hiding place, crying in the low guttural Egungun' khaa, khoo'. Death and his followers dropped the staff and fled in terror.

Amaiyeguti and his followers picked up their staffs and pursued them. As they overtook them, they struck them on the head. 'Gba!', one fell; 'Gba!' another fell. Since that time, Death and his followers have never returned to Ife (Lawal, 1977)."

This story emphasizes something we talked about earlier. In the first chapter, we spoke of how the Yoruba say Obatala was instructed to shape clay into human form. The Supreme Being breathed life into it. Thus, the Yoruba people believe that the human body is nothing but a mask, a sculpture for the person's soul to occupy. So when someone dies, their soul escapes the body and roams, no longer tethered. You can say the mask has slipped off.

That is why in these cultures, the likeness of someone, whether it is a figurine, effigy, picture, or mask, is considered serious and even dangerous to tamper with. The soul can be invited to inhabit your body, even momentarily, when disturbed. Even if that person is still alive.

They believe fate can be tethered to an object. Even an enemy can make a sculpture in your likeness or take a photograph of you and invite a part of your spirit to hurt you in real life. This is why people who participate in egungun are usually only possessed by spirits that have passed. The masks and costumes they wear, typically covered head to toe, invite the spirits from another realm to possess them and are often seen acting or imitating the people who have passed.

This also illuminates funeral proceedings. The Yoruba and others believe that when a person sheds their body (dies), they hang around and watch their own funeral proceedings. This is to inspect that everything is done correctly. Their graduation into the higher ranks of society is being respected and honored. After their body is buried, a second burial occurs where the person's likeness, in the form of a picture or wooden sculpture, is dressed in their finest clothes and paraded around the community and then buried. When that cannot be done, the next best thing is using their child who looks similar to them (it doesn't matter if the clothes fit or not). If the ceremony is deemed poor by the spirit, the spirit can stick around until their needs are met. This is an undesirable position because the spirit can cause chaos and torment you.

When a child is born who looks like the deceased or acts like them, it is believed that the spirit has returned. The reasons for this are not clear, but it isn't always because of unfinished business, as some like to think. If the child is the same sex as the deceased and a boy, they are called Babatunde (father returns), and Yetunde (mother returns) as a girl (Lawal, 1977).

Another thing that can be done to appease the spirit is to give them a chance to say goodbye to their loved ones. To do this, a random person would wear their clothes and put on a mask that resembles the spirit. This allows the spirit to possess them. Then they would go to the family: hug them, talk to them, and say goodbye.

So spirits, ancestral ones, are attracted to the form, possess, or come to life through "masks" that are familiar to them or are representative of them. This is why egungun works. That is where all their power lies. Women are not supposed to participate in the festivities, but they dress like men when they do.

A shrine can be built for the deceased. It would include a sculpture of the dead. It is believed when the people come to pray, offer sacrifices. So forth, the spirit of the deceased temporarily possesses the figure (Lawal, 1977).

FOUR

Vodun Itself

In this chapter, we will explore more details of Vodun, such as how it is practiced, how you pick your god, and other aspects of a more focused discussion.

An Oral Tradition

Vodun is shared through oral retellings. This means unlike other mainstream religions, there aren't holy books to study or reference. Although there have been some texts on Vodun supplemented in the 20th century, mostly in circumstances where Vodun is combined with Christianity.

There are many flying impressions of oral traditions in general. The most significant criticism is that they are changeable and cannot be trusted to be accurate or remain the same through the years. In contrast, the written word is seen as being more permanent and unchangeable. If changes are made, they are traceable.

But I believe it would be false to assume that the beliefs would lose their power or verifiability because of this aspect. Oral traditions are what allow Vodun to be adaptable, powerful, alluring, and relevant. All this has to do with the nature of oral traditions themselves.

Oral traditions have a way of discarding fluff, unnecessary detail to distill qualities and features that define and focus on the human experience (Scheub, 1985). In some of the stories, we saw how sparse they are in form and how much they manage to say. Because oral traditions universalize their message, removing it from its historical context allows them to find numerous applications in a wide variety of circumstances and periods (Scheub, 1985). Oral traditions shape these critical messages in memorable images that evoke strong emotions. This awakens the audience to old consciousness's that contain ancient wisdom and revelations.

So oral traditions aren't meant to capture how things actually occurred. Even if they manage to do so, it's not their primary purpose. Their power is to offer insight, commentary, and wisdom. They are meant to scrape, repackage and transmit all the knowledge and the revelation that accumulates through time and present them in a way that makes the most sense – in a way that is memorable and easy to digest.

Oral traditions are not only about sitting around a fire and telling tall tales. They come in a variety of ways. You will find riddles, lyrical poems, proverbs, and even animated performances or reenactments. In many circumstances, they are accompanied by music and theater-type lighting. These performances allow a blending of the past with the present, transporting the audience. The stories told to offer more perspective and metaphors like what we saw in the retelling of various Fon tales.

This fits perfectly within Vodun's ethos of dynamism,

connecting beyond oneself and being immersed in a world that is essentially populated by yore spirits. This allows for the merging and connection of various entities that are separated by distance and time. Oral traditions distill what is most important and meaningful and then threads all these communities together into a whole.

Temples and Worship

Before we delve into this section, it is worth reiterating something that will become important in making sense of the contents of this section. At the center of Vodun are many ideas. Still, the concepts of possession and gods manifesting themselves in the world play a crucial role. Nature and spirituality are intertwined, and the earth is under the gods' and goddesses' domain.

Choosing a God

Vodun is often characterized by others as virtually a practical religion, meaning believers expect to be helped in this lifetime. We can see how this contrasts with Christianity; for example, in Christianity, there is an emphasis—at least in most denominations—on getting into heaven. There seems to be an impression that life is just a stop before death. This is not an attitude you will find in West African religions like Vodun, and you can now see why. If the entire idea behind existence is happening in the same space (no separation between the living and dead), then there is no "next life," only a continuance of this life. So when deciding on a god to follow, this factor plays a significant role.

People choose a god to meet real-world needs like protection for themselves, for good luck, family, blessings, and thank the god when they have been blessed or appease a god they believe has been offended. They worship a god whom they think will better serve their interests and ambitions. For instance, blacksmiths may worship Gu, who is the god of iron and war (who we have established is much more than that). Sometimes, when an individual or family finds themselves in a challenging position, they might worship a god they think will help them in that particular situation. A person who is ill might pray and make sacrifices to Age as they take the medicine they need.

There is a specialization within the gods. The number of gods in Vodun keeps increasing and becoming more and more particular. You might find a god who is skilled at healing in general and one who deals with specific health problems like gout.

Another aspect that determines what gods a person or people are going to follow is God's requirements. For instance, some gods are thought to be strict, highly demanding, or temperamental. Still, when met, they are more likely to deliver. These types of gods are usually more expensive, monetarily, and otherwise, and difficult to please, so some people may be discouraged from worshiping them. These stringent gods might only be consulted when they considered the only solution to the problem. While those gods who are considered more versatile and approachable might gain a more considerable following in communities, it is easy for most people in the community to meet their demands and hear from them.

Another factor that determines what a community or person will devote most of its resources to is the profession, and I alluded to this earlier. A particular trade guild may have a certain god as its patron. For instance, fishermen may have Agbe as their patron god because he watches over the seas and fish. This, however, does not mean that those in that profession have to only worship that god (Cults and Rituals, n.d.).

This brings us to one of the most fascinating aspects of Vodun and many other polytheistic religions. The adherents of that belief do not have to dedicate their lives to one god alone. They are free (not always with ease) to switch and serve multiple gods according to their personal needs and situation. Again, we are seeing versatility and adaptability.

Another aspect that plays a role in whether an individual worships a particular god is gender. Some gods are considered feminine, and others are considered masculine. Feminine gods attract a majority of women, and masculine gods attract men. Interestingly some gods are sexless or are ambiguous. Men who worship gods considered feminine usually have to wear dresses to worship that god, and vice versa with the women who worship gods that are considered masculine.

Another major factor that plays a role in what god a person chooses to worship is family. So if you come from a family that has always revered a certain god, you might decide to follow that one because it's what you know from growing up. There is an affinity there. If your family has been incredibly well off under a particular god, members of that family see that as a sign of favor. There is no telling what will happen if they profess allegiance to another god. The god they turn to might not return the favor or the god they abandon might be offended and cause them harm. Either way, it is not a risk worth taking. The only exception to this is if a woman marries into another family. When that happens, the woman may worship the god of their in-laws, but after marriage, she is expected to also return to the god of her father's house.

There are also communal reasons for choosing particular gods. Some groups may think of themselves as primarily serving one specific god. Individuals in that community may need to pledge allegiance to that god while still worshipping other gods who are more personal and familial (Cults and Rituals, n.d.). Community gods are prayed to and served through community priests and collectively when the time is right.

Gods may also recruit people they want. Gods do this in various ways: they can send messages in a dream, send signs, give the person a problem or trouble them (Cults and Rituals, n.d.). When they consult a Vodun practitioner, they will be told that the god wants their allegiance. For instance, a person might suffer from fits. When they consult a Fa practitioner, they might be told that a certain god wants their attention, a sacrifice, or allegiance, and their illness will be cured or alleviated if they do.

Ceremonies

We have already established that Vodun is a widespread religion in West Africa and the African diaspora, primarily because of the slave trade. Because of the distance and the versatile nature of Vodun, it has evolved in some ways that are particular to specific regions. Still, overall it has retained a lot of the same convictions and practices. That is why we will use Haitian Vodun to talk about and explore the topic of temples and worship. Keep in mind that not everything here will be the same everywhere you go. You will find different iterations of the exact details depending on the place you find yourself or the person you consult. This is to be expected.

A Vodun temple can either be a separate building or a smaller structure behind a house. The official name for a Vodun temple is hounfour, humbo, or ounphor (Guiley,

1999). Within it, there is an altar, and in some cases, you will find nooks or rooms that initiates can use for meditation. On the altar is a stone called pe, which holds candles and small jars. These little jars are called govis, and they contain ancestral spirits. The temple is decorated in veves, symbols that represent the gods. These symbols are intricate, beautiful, and bear a magic aura about them. They represent the vodun who is being worshipped there. Offerings may be made at the altar in the form of money, drink, food, charms, ritual rattles, sacred stones, and other items.

Outside the temple is a roofed or low wall encircled courtyard called peristyle. The temple itself is usually small and cannot house all the ceremony participants. Hence, most gather in the peristyle, and a lot of the traditions take place there. A person who is not appropriately dressed cannot be permitted into the peristyle. Still, they can watch from outside the peristyle since it is low-walled (spectatorship is allowed). The floor of the peristyle is usually made with packed earth. If there is one, the center post also has powerful decorations on it that represent the spiritual power of voduns and has magical powers. It is usually decorated with squares, circles, crosses, and triangles, and it represents Mawu's serpent that holds the worlds together (Guiley, 1999).

Further out, trees are surrounding the courtyard, and these are sanctuaries for the gods. Because of the close connection between nature and the gods, these trees are a physical expression of the gods, and offerings are often made to them in drink, food, and money.

The gathering reaches its height when vodun begins possessing those gathered (not all of them, mostly the chosen or the initiated). Possession has taken place when the spirit has taken over a person's mind and body, making the person lose consciousness. This shows itself in various ways: they dance and frolic with no awareness, slump over and appear disabled. Their expression may contort, and they might act in ways that are uncharacteristic and devoid of self-consciousness. The vodun takes this opportunity to address the gathering and perform services for them. They punish or protect; grant skills and talents; give prophecies; perform healings; exorcise evil spirits. Take offerings and assists in rituals; provide advice and counsel; make revelations.

The priests are called houngan, and the priestesses are called mambo. Their job is to invite the vodun and expel them when they are done with their business. Their authority and roles come from the voduns themselves. They also function as diviners, healers, counselors, and spiritual leaders. They use a rattle called an asson made from calabash to summon the vodun and other spirits. The asson is decorated to symbolize ancestor gods and the serpent Aida-Hwedo. Once they have used these symbols to attract vodun, additional actions are performed. Shaking the asson or striking it with a god's symbol to release their power and incorporate them into the ceremony.

Other members that are important to the ceremony are called Laplace. They coordinate the singing, chanting, drum beating, and flag-waving, and other activities. They usually carry the ritual sword, which is also decorated with powerful sigils. The sword's name, Ku-bah-sah, means "cutting away all that is material" (Guiley, 1999). The Laplace swings the sword east to west, cutting all that is material, so worshipers can come into the charged divine place. Initiates are the ones who get sacrificial animals and are charged with preparing them, and they also oversee their distribution.

FIVE

Society and Culture

WE ARE GOING TO LOOK AT SOME PAST AND PRESENT cultural aspects of West African societies. These are the ones I find the most interesting and curated for you to get a better picture. I believe they provide more in-depth knowledge and appreciation of the region. There is always more to learn and explore the region beyond what I present here, and I hope it sparks an interest that you pursue further.

Amazon Warriors

The Kingdom of Dahomey existed between 1600 to 1904. It was the Fon kingdom and the main reason why Vodun has spread so far across the world. Dahomey was one of the most important and influential powers in West Africa. It built its economy on conquest, slave labor and trade with European powers, and other typical ways states raise money like taxation. In their dealing with Europeans, they exchanged war prisoners, petty criminals, and others for a host of goods like bayonets, knives, firearms, fabric, and alcohol. Dahomey was popular with Europeans because of the all-female military unit, which they referred to as the Amazons, and for Dahomey's annual human sacrifice practice (usually prisoners or criminals). At the time, the sight of an all-female military unit was shocking and exciting for outsiders. It shattered perceptions held by men that women were frail, weak, and needed protection.

In African societies, the roles of women varied from culture to culture, with some similarities. Tasks were usually divided along gender lines despite having greater flexibility than the much more rigid definition of women's role in European societies. This explains why the formation of a women-only army was more comfortable for Dahomey rulers to accept, even if women were not permitted to join the military.

It is believed that the Dahomey Amazons may have come from gbetos, female hunters who specialized in hunting elephants. Already, we see much more flexible gender roles than you would at the time in Europe or modern society in general. As the numbers of elephants dwindled, the gbeto stopped hunting and turned their expertise to meet the palace's food and sacrificial animals' needs. The gbeto were an interesting bunch, dressed in brown shirts and knee-length trousers with antelope horns attached above their forehead on an iron or gold ring. It is said that there were four hundred of them who remained elite warriors until disbanding (Dahomey, Women Warriors/Wives of the King, 2000).

The first record of women in the Dahomey army is from 1708. King Adja was short of men but wanted to expand his kingdom and gain access to the international slave trade (Dahomey, Women Warriors/Wives of the King, 2000). He recruited women into the army, and to his surprise, they exceeded expectations. He expanded this women-only military unit to upwards of two thousand. Some of them served as his personal guard. His successors would continue this tradition of women in their forces and guardianships for decades. As soldiers, the woman wore sleeveless waistcoats with trousers and hats decorated with crocodiles. There are some pictures and illustrations of the women wearing long skirts, brandishing blunderbusses, muskets, bows and arrows, and spear-like poles.

Women were recruited into the army in several ways, either by volunteers, drafting soldiers, or trading for POW's, slaves, or members of misaligned groups. The concept of the soldier slave is not a new construct. By then, Islamic powers had been using slaves to wage wars against their enemies for centuries. For Western Africa, this would be well known. Women combatants reveal about Dahomey as an extraordinary pragmatism and resourcefulness; as an expansionary power, they needed to take opportunities to present themselves. Misaligned groups that were integrated into the army unit were adulterous or rebels from the state.

The Dahomey Amazons were known to be self-right-eous and celebrate their discipline. These women were proud of the position they held in society. However, to fit in the military culture that was still male-dominated, they had to cultivate a masculine appearance. Their sex life was complicated. Celibacy was required, but as we know from history, this is not always a rule that is strictly followed. For instance, the women were given amenorrhea-causing contraceptives, so if they had sex, they would not get pregnant. And if they got pregnant, the women were punished. Although the women were close to the king and even fought to the death to protect him, they were not intimate despite having the nickname "Wives of The King." In rare circumstances, marriages between a king and soldier occurred (two on record).

The Amazon warriors of Dahomey helped overturn some long-held ideas about women, especially for Europeans who wrote and spoke about them with passion.

Gelede Festival

The Gelede festival is a spectacle of masks and ritual dance by the Yoruba people. It was beginning to honor Mother Nature, increase the fertility of the tribe, prevent premature death, and promote social cohesion and worship. The festival also honors mothers in all forms, such as the ancestors and goddesses. It also celebrates the social and spiritual power of women. There are spiritually aggressive and non-aggressive ways of achieving this goal. Gelede is thought to be a non-aggressive way of doing so. It is taken from a line in a Yoruba adage that says, "The world is fragile." The saying suggested that the world and life are unpredictable and delicate, and care must be taken for positive outcomes. Aggression is regarded as a force that cannot be safely administered because it breaks things down. This is why you often hear, "Anything handled with care becomes easier, anything handled with force becomes harder" (Babatunde Lawal, 1996).

Gelede visual arts and performances do this with sarcastic humor to create a calm, fun atmosphere that enables them to deal with sensitive topics without inflaming tensions. Social harmony is encouraged through the participation of both men and women in the festival, despite there being many women in the society. These numbers are explained by the belief that the festival promotes fertility within society. The fertility that is being promulgated is not only for women but also for men. Various Gelede societies appoint officials, groups, and other personnel to oversee performance and the community itself. Each Gelede society's structure contains roughly an Iyalase, Bbalase, Abore, Elfer, Arugi, and Onilu.

The Iyalase is the Chief Priestess, also known as the mother of the shrine and head of the Gelede society. This means she is the main person of contact between the Supreme Being and society. Her studies include running the Gelede shrine, Ase, where she is the only person allowed. They are the most privileged member of the Gelede society.

The Babablase is the shrine's father. Their main job is organizing events, keeping headdress, costumes and ensuring coordination of different parts of the organizations. The Babablase works as an assistant to the Iyalase. They are appointed by her and the powerful mothers. The Abore is the male priest that helps people who need help with the aje, a female god with special powers, for rituals. In some cases, the position of Abore is hereditary, requiring a plethora of knowledge on traditions and esoteric aspects of the society.

The Elelfe are primarily humorists. The man must be older, have a rich knowledge of oral literature and the community. They are tasked with praying for prosperity to the community and promote building behavior. Going against their teaching is unacceptable. The Arugi is the masker; they must be good dancers and well versed in proverbs, language, and attuned to the drums. The Arugi are trained at a young age when they appear to have talent. They are given masks and perform for the community in the annual Gelede festival. The Onilu are the drummers or experts of music, and the Agberin are a chorus of men and women (Babatunde Lawal, 1996).

Looking closely, you can see that the Gelede festival has some elements of Egungun, the usage of masks. But the two are different in their emphasis. Egungun is primarily a spiritual event, where spirits possess people; Gelede is mainly a communal event that coaxes the gods for goodwill. Egungun is considered aggressive and dangerous by some, whereas the Gelede festival is much more festive and joyful. While the two can foster social cohesion and set the community's direction or even engender goodwill of the gods and ancestors, they do so in starkly different ways, guided by other philosophies.

Voodoo Festival of Benin

The Voodoo Festival of Benin takes place annually, always in the first month of the year. Voodoo is another word for Vodun, but I avoided using the term for obvious negative connotations. The word voodoo is one of the ways that people like to demonize and caricature the Vodun religion. The festival, among other things, is about reappropriating the term and dispelling these negative connotations. The festival celebrates the diversity of the Vodun religion, ancestral cults, and traditional leaders.

People participating leave the Temple of Pythons and walk or ride in a parade along an ancient slave route to the beach where the festival commences. The atmosphere is vibrant. There is drum beating, dancing, people acting possessed by spirits, singing, and other eye capturing displays of culture. People are dressed in colorful, elaborate costumes representing gods, cults, sects, ancestors, spirits, or figures from old stories.

The Voodoo festival is a joyful affair. Tourists come from all over the world to watch and witness this spectacle. The festival reaches its climax with the arrival of the priest of Quidah.

International Festival of the Dahomean Culture

Held every year during December, the International Festival of the Dahomean Culture lasts ten days. It takes place in Abomey Benin and celebrates the diversity of Benin.

The atmosphere is festive. There are different traditional costumes, songs, and dances, the performance of various folk songs and stories of the Dahomey Kingdom from which Benin originates. Because of the intertwined history with neighboring countries, the festival attracts spectators from other West African regions.

Conclusion

We started this journey of West African spirituality by contrasting how God's concepts in this region are different from those of the Christian faith. We noted that in many religions like Christianity, God often interferes in this creation's lives with somewhat clear intentions. West African conceptions of the Supreme Being, their version of God, give us a figure that does not interfere with their creative lives. The Supreme Being leaves such tasks to the lesser gods that descend from them or are objects of creation. Furthermore, the Supreme Being has no specific plans for humanity. It is often not the subject of worship, although always revered or held to a higher standard of being.

We then saw the various concepts of Supreme Beings from West African cultures. From the retellings, some of them became involved in the lives of their creation, but in most conceptions, they stayed neutral. This led us to discuss the place of humans in the world according to West African traditions. Religion here is not distinguished between the physical and the spiritual. It is believed that all things are made the same. Therefore spiritual and physical do not have meaningful distinctions. Those distinctions only explain our experiences but not anything fundamental about the world.

We also learned that people here are left to make what they will of life, with no specific goal to attain eternal life or avoid eternal damnation. In our discussion of ancestral spirits, we highlight that West African communities don't consider death to transports us to another world, and there is no separation between the living and the dead. Instead, the two inhabit the same world, albeit in different levels of awareness.

We learned that Vodun, more popularly known as Voodoo, refers to the Fon people's Dahomenian religion, which spread across the globe through the slave trade. We learned that the name also refers to gods and goddesses of the Vodun religion, who are also called Loa or Lwa inside Vodun versions that have been promulgated in the American continent. We learned about these gods and the various roles in people's lives, and how they manifest in the world. Vodun were only a small fraction of the pantheon, but they were the most popular. The Yoruba tradition of Egungun functioned to illustrate just how central the belief is in West African communities and families.

Having discussed several gods, it was worth looking at Vodun itself. We noted a tradition shared through oral retellings and stories, with some texts eventually appearing in the 20th century. We talked about the complexities and reasoning behind following a particular god instead of another. It was here we spoke of the practical nature of Vodun as opposed to afterlife-orientated religions. For instance, prosperity in this life takes precedence in many of the religious decisions West Africans make. This does not make them any less in tune with their spirituality. One would argue this pragmatism inspired these cultures to include their beliefs in almost every decision because the gods they worship are still very much of this world. We also looked at an example of a Vodun ceremony using Haitian Vodun as an example.

We spent a brief time on the culture and society of West Africans. We talked about the Amazon at length and briefly about the festivals that celebrate diversity, culture, and shared history, all very important for a well-rounded picture of this society.

Religious Changes

It is difficult to track the changes that happen in Vodun, and differences become apparent once many of them have already occurred. We have seen how Vodun's emphasis on versatility, pragmatism, and adaptability are forces that enable it to keep taking new forms and changing with time. As it stands, Vodun has morphed over the centuries, and it will continue to change as long as humans walk the earth, progress, and their needs evolve. And that will not be anathema to the religion's tenets. Its gods change and develop and grow, allowing communities to hold on to them even in trying times. In this way, Vodun and other West African religions are forever because they resemble the universe's fabric. It follows the same set of rules everywhere while allowing for significant variations.

References

Babatunde Lawal. (1996). The Gèlèdé spectacle : art, gender, and social harmony in an African culture. University Of Washington Press.

Belcher, S. (2005). African myths of origin. Penguin Books.

Cults and Rituals. (n.d.). Encyclopedia. https://www.encyclopedia.com/history/news-wires-white-papers-and-books/cults-and-rituals

Dahomey, Women Warriors/Wives of the King. (2000). Encyclopedia. https://www.encyclopedia.com/social-sciences/encyclopedias-almanacs-transcripts-and-maps/dahomey-women-warriorswives-king

Folly, Y. (2020, January 12). Benin celebrates West African voodoo – in pictures. The Guardian. https://www.theguardian.-com/world/gallery/2020/jan/12/benin-celebrates-west-african-voodoo-in-pictures

God: African Supreme Beings. (n.d.). Encyclopedia. https://www.encyclopedia.com/environment/encyclopedias-almanacs-transcripts-and-maps/god-african-supreme-beings

Guiley, R. (1999). The encyclopedia of witches and witchcraft. Checkmark Books.

Lawal, B. (1977). The Living Dead: Art and Immortality among the Yoruba of Nigeria. Africa, 47(1), 50–61. https://doi.org/10.2307/1159194

Mbiti, J. S. (1994). Introduction to African religion. Nairobi East African Educational Publ.

Peter Van Inwagen. (2015). Metaphysics. Westview Press.

Scheub, H. (1985). A Review of African Oral Traditions and Literature. African Studies Review, 28(2/3), 1. https://doi.org/10.2307/524603

Vodun (Voodoo) (n.d.). Encyclopedia. https://www.encyclopedia.com/religion/legal-and-political-magazines/vodun-voodoo

West African Religions. (n.d.). Encyclopedia. https://www.encyclopedia.com/environment/encyclopedias-almanacs-transcripts-and-maps/west-african-religions

More Books by Monique Joiner Siedlak

Practical Magick
 Wiccan Basics
 Candle Magick
 Wiccan Spells
 Love Spells
 Abundance Spells
 Herb Magick
 Moon Magick
 Creating Your Own Spells
 Gypsy Magic
 Protection Magick
 Celtic Magick

Personal and Self Development
 Creative Visualization
 Astral Projection for Beginners
 Meditation for Beginners
 Reiki for Beginners
 Manifesting With the Law of Attraction

Stress Management
Being an Empath Today

Get a Handle on Life
Get a Handle on Anxiety
Get a Handle on Depression
Get a Handle on Procrastination

The Yoga Collective
Yoga for Beginners
Yoga for Stress
Yoga for Back Pain
Yoga for Weight Loss
Yoga for Flexibility
Yoga for Advanced Beginners
Yoga for Fitness
Yoga for Runners
Yoga for Energy
Yoga for Your Sex Life
Yoga To Beat Depression and Anxiety
Yoga for Menstruation
Yoga to Detox Your Body
Yoga to Tone Your Body

A Natural Beautiful You
Creating Your Own Body Butter
Creating Your Own Body Scrub
Creating Your Own Body Spray

THANK YOU FOR READING MY BOOK! I REALLY APPRECIATE ALL OF YOUR FEEDBACK AND I LOVE TO HEAR WHAT YOU HAVE TO SAY. PLEASE LEAVE YOUR REVIEW AT YOUR FAVORITE RETAILER!

www.ingramcontent.com/pod-product-compliance
Lightning Source LLC
Chambersburg PA
CBHW060423050426

42449CB00009B/2098